DAY
1

BELIEVE THAT GOD WANTS YOU TO PROSPER.

☐ One of the many names of God is Jehovah-Jireh, "God will Provide." Never doubt the giving nature of your Father.

☐ *You matter* to him. Your *needs* matter to him. Every *desire* of your heart is important to him.

☐ Your total prosperity is on His mind all the time.

WISDOM FROM THE WORD

"Let them shout for joy, and be glad, that favour my righteous cause: yea, let them say continually, Let the Lord be magnified, which hath pleasure in the prosperity of his servant."

Psalm 35:27

S0-DVD-534

DAY
2

EMBRACE TRUE PROSPERITY.

❑ Don't misunderstand "prosperity." Your *future* depends on it.

❑ Let's define it. Prosperity is simply *having enough of God's provisions to complete His instructions for your life.*

❑ Prosperity increases your ability to bless others.

WISDOM FROM THE WORD

"Beloved, I wish above all things that thou mayest prosper and be in health, even as thy soul prospereth."
III John 1:2

DAY
3

WASH YOUR MIND WITH THE WORD.

❑ The Bible is God's Blueprint for mankind. It defines His purpose for creating, as well as His covenant to bless us.

❑ God promised that meditation on His words would produce the miracle of prosperity.

❑ *Nothing will ever dominate your life that doesn't happen daily.* (So, meditate on His Word, daily.)

❑ One of your great discoveries will be the Principle of Seed-Faith.

WISDOM FROM THE WORD

"That he might sanctify and cleanse it with the washing of water by the word."
Ephesians 5:26
"Keep therefore the words of this covenant, and do them, that ye may prosper in all that ye do."
Deuteronomy 29:9

DAY
4

RESPECT THE LAW OF SOWING AND REAPING.

❑ When a farmer plants corn, he reaps corn. When he plants apple seeds, he produces more apples.

❑ When you sow love, you will reap love. If you sow hatred, you will reap the harvest of hatred.

❑ This Scriptural Law of Sowing and Reaping is *universal*. Fools *deny* it. Rebels *defy* it. The wise *live by it*.

WISDOM FROM THE WORD

"Be not deceived, God is not mocked: for whatsoever a man soweth, that shall he also reap."
Galatians 6:7

DAY
5

UNLOCK YOUR FUTURE.

- ❑ Seed-Faith is *exchanging* what you have been *given* for what God has *promised* you.

- ❑ Seed-Faith is sowing a Seed *in faith* for a specific Harvest.

- ❑ Seed-Faith *pulls the Future toward you.*

WISDOM FROM THE WORD

"Give, and it shall be given unto you; good measure, pressed down, and shaken together, and running over, shall men give into your bosom. For with the same measure that ye mete withal it shall be measured to you again."
Luke 6:38

DAY
6

NAME YOUR SEED.

❏ Inventory your *total* possessions.

❏ Everyone has *something* to give or sow.

❏ Your seed is anything you have that will benefit another person, your *smile*... a *word* of encouragement... *time*... shared *information*... *money*.

WISDOM FROM THE WORD

"As every man hath received the gift, even so minister the same one to another, as good stewards of the manifold grace of God."
I Peter 4:10

DAY
7

GET EXCITED ABOUT YOUR HUNDRED-FOLD RETURN.

❑ Jesus always promised a reward for any act of obedience.

❑ Start sowing your seed with expectation of His blessing.

❑ Don't treat the promise of "Hundred-Fold" return lightly. It is your Father's opportunity to celebrate your Faith.

WISDOM FROM THE WORD

"And Jesus answered and said, Verily I say unto you, There is no man that hath left house, or brethren, or sisters, or father, or mother, or wife, or children, or lands, for my sake, and the gospels. But he shall receive an hundredfold now in this time, houses, and brethren, and sisters, and mothers, and children, and lands, with persecutions; and in the world to come eternal life."
Mark 10:29, 30

DAY
8

ASK FOR A SPECIFIC HARVEST.

☐ Your Seed is whatever you give to God.

☐ Your Harvest is whatever God gives to you.

☐ Name the particular miracle you want from God.

WISDOM FROM THE WORD

"...But in every thing by prayer and supplication with thanksgiving let your requests be made known unto God."
Philippians 4:6

DAY
9

RECOGNIZE YOUR HARVEST.

❑ Your harvest is any *person* or *anything* that can bless or benefit you.

❑ It may be someone who can *contribute* something to you that you *need*... information... favor ... finances..., or it can be an explosive *idea*.

❑ Your harvest *already* exists. It is walking around you! Just as your eyes had to be opened to recognize *Jesus*, your eyes must be opened to recognize your *harvest*.

WISDOM FROM THE WORD

"He was in the world, and the world was made by him, and the world knew him not. He came unto his own, and his own received him not.
John 1:10, 11

DAY
10

RECOGNIZE YOUR SEED.

❑ Your Seed is any gift, skill, or talent that God has provided for you, to sow into the lives of others.

❑ Don't hide it. *Use* it. Celebrate it. It carves the road to your future.

❑ Even Joseph wanted others to recognize his ability to interpret dreams.

WISDOM FROM THE WORD

"A man's gift maketh room for him, and bringeth him before great men."
Proverbs 18:16

DAY
11

START GIVING YOUR WAY OUT OF TROUBLE.

❑ Your Seed is always your *bridge* out of trouble.

❑ The widow of Zarephath used her Seed to create a harvest in the midst of a famine. Joseph used his gift of interpreting dreams to catapult himself from the prison to the palace.

❑ *Whatever God has placed in your hand is always enough to get you out of trouble.*

WISDOM FROM THE WORD

"Neglect not the gift that is in thee, which was given thee by prophesy, with the laying on of the hands of the presbytery."
I Timothy 4:14

DAY
12

HONOR THE TITHE.

☐ Tithing is the Biblical practice of *returning* ten percent of your income back to God after you have earned it.

☐ In the Old Testament, Abraham tithed. In the New Testament, even the Pharisees' tithing was noted by Jesus.

☐ Make God your financial partner. *Make every payday a Seed-Sowing Day.* Results are *guaranteed*.

WISDOM FROM THE WORD

"And all the tithe of the land, whether of the seed of the land, or of the fruit of the tree, is the Lord's: it is holy unto the Lord... And concerning the tithe of the herd, or of the flock, even of whatsoever passeth under the rod, the tenth shall be holy unto the Lord."

Leviticus 27:30, 32

DAY
13

PAY YOUR VOWS.

❏ Always honor your promises to the Lord. It is also important that you honor your word to those in your family or business transactions.

❏ God is a Covenant-God. He seriously weighs every vow you have made before Him or man.

❏ Stop. Re-examine your past vows. Pay them. It positions you for *reward*.

WISDOM FROM THE WORD

"When thou vowest a vow unto God, defer not to pay it; for he hath no pleasure in fools: pay that which thou hast vowed. Better is it that thou shouldest not vow, than that thou shouldest vow and not pay."
Ecclesiastes 5:4, 5

DAY
14

BREAK THE FINANCIAL CURSE.

- ❑ Those who rob God of the tithe and offerings that belong to Him live under a curse.

- ❑ *You can break "the Curse."* As you sow today, remember that your Seed is proof that you have conquered greed.

- ❑ God penalizes a thief, but always promotes and prospers the Seed-Sower.

WISDOM FROM THE WORD

"Will a man rob God? Yet ye have robbed me. But ye say, Wherein have we robbed thee? In tithes an offerings. Ye are cursed with a curse: for ye have robbed me, even this whole nation. Bring ye all the tithes into the storehouse, that there may be meat in mine house, and prove me now herewith, saith the Lord of hosts, if I will not open you the windows of heaven, and pour you out a blessing, that there shall not be room enough to receive it."
Malachi 3:8-10

DAY
15

OPEN YOUR HAND AND GOD WILL OPEN HIS HAND.

❑ Whatever you have in *your* hand is a Seed, Whatever God has in *His hand* is your Harvest.

❑ Nothing leaves Heaven until something leaves earth.

❑ Don't let fear and unbelief make you close your hands and hoard. Open your hands today and God will pour out the greatest blessings you have ever experienced.

WISDOM FROM THE WORD

"Bring ye all the tithes into the storehouse, that there may be meat in mine house, and prove me now herewith, saith the Lord of hosts, if I will not open you the windows of heaven, and pour you out a blessing, that there shall not be room enough to receive it. And I will rebuke the devourer for your sakes, and he shall not destroy the fruits of your ground; neither shall your vine cast her fruit before the time in the field, saith the Lord of hosts." Malachi 3:10, 11

DAY
16

RELEASE THE HOLY SPIRIT TO BRING YOUR HARVEST.

❑ The Holy Spirit can *go* where you cannot go. The Holy Spirit can say what you cannot *say*. The Holy Spirit can *do* what you cannot do.

❑ You can pray in your city... the Holy Spirit will talk to someone 2,000 miles away.

❑ *Honor the Holy Spirit*. Permit Him to *move*. don't quench Him. He is the *movement* of the Seed-faith principle.

WISDOM FROM THE WORD

"That they should seek the Lord, if haply they might feel after him, and find him, though he be not far from every one of us: For in him we live, and move, and have our being; as certain also of your own poets have said, For we are also his offspring." Acts 17:27,28

DAY
17

TAKE THE LIMITS OFF OF GOD.

❑ *Anytime you attempt to do the Impossible, you will create a crisis.* These are the seasons that pleasure God... for this allows him to *reveal* Himself... His power... and His love.

❑ *You serve a big God... so, make BIG plans.* He delights in *proving* His power to you.

❑ This is the secret of Seed-faith: Whatever you have in your hand is what God will use to create your future. *Don't limit God.* ANYTHING IS POSSIBLE.

WISDOM FROM THE WORD

"...But the people that do know their God shall be strong, and do exploits."
Daniel 11:32b

DAY
18

DON'T TOLERATE LACK.

- ❏ Poverty is *wrenching*... Torturous... Tormenting. It strips a person of the ability to give... to bless... to make a contribution to others. *Don't tolerate it.*

- ❏ Learn to despise lack. *You will never conquer what you cannot hate.*

- ❏ Your Seed is the *Enemy of Lack.* It is the *only* proof that you truly desire a Harvest.

WISDOM FROM THE WORD

"And God is able to make all grace abound toward you; that ye, always having all sufficiency in all things, may abound to every good work."
II Corinthians 9:8

DAY
19

EXPLORE NEW INCOME POSSIBILITIES.

❏ You are *not* locked into your present job. You have *chosen* to be where you are. you can *choose* to be somewhere else.

❏ *Seasons* change. *Companies* change. *You* change. *Accept it.* Enjoy your God-given right to creatively pursue and explore other job opportunities.

❏ Most assignments are *seasonal*. Permit God to walk you into the *next* chapter of success in your life.

WISDOM FROM THE WORD

"Behold, I will do a new thing; now it shall spring forth; shall ye not know it? I will even make a way in the wilderness, and rivers in the desert."
Isaiah 43:19

DAY
20

BUILD YOUR BUDGET WITH FAITH.

❑ Your budget is simply a *written* Plan for Spending. It is the secret of every Financial Champion.

❑ Your Financial World is decided by three factors: (1) what you *spend*, (2) what you *save*, and (3) what you *sow*.

❑ When you put God *first* in tithes an offerings, you are building your budget on a Foundation of *Faith*... for the *Rest* of your needs to be met.

WISDOM FROM THE WORD

"But seek ye first the kingdom of God, and his righteousness; and all these things shall be added unto you."
Matthew 6:33

DAY
21

ACCEPT THE SEED THAT GOD SOWED.

- ❏ God had a Son. He wanted a *family*. Like a Seed, He planted His Son. The place was called *Calvary*.

- ❏ God lost what He loved... *for a Season*, to produce *more* of what He loved... you and me.

- ❏ Jesus is the Seed within you that reproduces the nature of God. Accept Him now as Saviour... Lord... King of your life.

WISDOM FROM THE WORD

"For ye know the grace of our Lord Jesus Christ, that, though he was rich, yet for your sakes he became poor, that ye through his poverty might be rich."
II Corinthians 8:9

DAY
22

BECOME SOMEONE'S HARVEST.

- ❑ *What you are, you will reproduce around you*. The Irishman produces Irishmen. The apple produces more apples. The giver creates giver... who wants to contribute into his life.

- ❑ What appears to be a *loss* today will prove to be a *gain* tomorrow.

- ❑ *You are a Seed*. Sow yourself into the future. Sow yourself into someone else. You are somebody's harvest today. Find them.

WISDOM FROM THE WORD

"Give, and it shall be given unto you; good measure, pressed down, and shaken together, and running over, shall men give into your bosom. For with the same measure that ye mete withal it shall be measured to you again."

Luke 6:38

DAY
23

GIVE YOURSELF AWAY.

❑ You are a collection of *parts*. When you sow a *part* of yourself back in God's world, you activate the *Law of Increase*.

❑ Sow extra *time* into your family and you will see an *increase* of love and affection. Sow the Seed of *diligence* into your job and you will be *promoted*.

❑ Start giving yourself away. After all, *everything you have was given to you*.

WISDOM FROM THE WORD

"Heal the sick, cleanse the lepers, raise the dead, cast out devils: freely ye have received, freely give."
Matthew 10:8

DAY
24

FIND SOMEBODY IN TROUBLE.

☐ *Everyone hurts somewhere.*

☐ You are oil for someone's wounds. You are the map for someone who is lost. *Find them. God is always willing to become to you, whatever you are willing to become to another.*

☐ Remember you are a Seed. Sow yourself. Never forget: *What you make happen for others, God will make happen for you.*

WISDOM FROM THE WORD

"And if thou draw out thy soul to the hungry, and satisfy the afflicted soul; then shall thy light rise in obscurity, and thy darkness be as the noon day: And the Lord shall guide thee continually, and satisfy thy soul in drought, and make fat thy bones: and thou shalt be like a watered garden, and like a spring of water, whose waters fail not." Isaiah 58:10, 11

DAY
25

SOW MERCY; EXPECT MERCY.

☐ *Forgiveness is a Seed.* Sow it generously, and you will reap it generously.

☐ Each offense from others is actually an *opportunity.* It is your chance to create *favor* with man... and, God.

☐ *Your Heavenly Father will never give to you what you refuse to give to others.* Mercy-People *attract* mercy into their lives.

WISDOM FROM THE WORD

"For if ye forgive men their trespasses, your heavenly Father will also forgive you: But if ye forgive not men their trespasses, neither will your Father forgive your trespasses."
Matthew 6:14, 15

DAY
26

FIGHT FOR YOUR HARVEST.

❑ You have an Enemy. An Adversary. A Thief. Satan wants to steal everything God has for you Don't let him!

❑ Use your weapons, to go after the harvest when it has been delayed. Your *weapons* are the *Word of God*, your *words*, and your *faith*.

❑ God *responds* to a fighter. Satan *fears* a fighter. *Every harvest in your life will require a battle.*

WISDOM FROM THE WORD

"Blessed be the Lord my strength, which teacheth my hands to war, and my fingers to fight."
Psalm 144:1

DAY
27

START CREATING TOMORROW... TODAY.

- ❑ A farmer begins sowing his seeds months *before* he needs the harvest. There is a *time* for *sowing*... a *time* for *reaping*.

- ❑ Tomorrow is being decided right now. Your Seeds of love... mercy... money... are *moving into your future*.

- ❑ *The Seed that leaves your hand will never leave your life.* It merely leaves your *present* season, and *enters your future* where it multiplies.

WISDOM FROM THE WORD

"To every thing there is a season, and a time to every purpose under the heaven: A time to be born, and a time to die; a time to plant, and a time to pluck up that which is planted...." Ecclesiastes 3:1, 2

DAY
28

DON'T FORGET YOUR SOURCE.

❏ Everything you need comes *from* God... *through* people. He is your Source. Men are His *channels*.

❏ God may use various people to benefit you. But, never forget to be thankful to the True Source - your Heavenly Father.

❏ *Read* the word of God aloud. *Speak* it aloud. It builds your confidence and faith in God.

WISDOM FROM THE WORD

"But without faith it is impossible to please him; for he that cometh to God must believe that he is, and that he is a rewarder of them that diligently seek him."
Hebrews 11:6

DAY
29

ESTABLISH A RHYTHM IN YOUR SOWING AND REAPING.

❑ Acknowledge the Fact of the Seasons...
Winter, Spring, Summer, Fall.
Regularity and routine are very
important forces in your life...
especially, in a Seed-Faith lifestyle.

❑ Your life is an endless cycle of sowing
and reaping; giving and receiving.
Work with it. Don't be erratic and
unpredictable. Nature itself has a
rhythm... a pattern. Honor it.

❑ Create a personal schedule for sowing
your finances into God's work. This
will create a *rhythm* and *consistency* in
the harvest you receive from God.

WISDOM FROM THE WORD

*"While the earth remaineth, seedtime and
harvest, and cold and heat, and summer
and winter, and day and night shall
not cease."* Genesis 8:22

DAY
30

CONQUER GREED.

❑ Satan *steals*. Man *hoards*. God *gives*. Your giving is the only proof that God lives within you. Whether it is money, mercy or love. *Giving is the only real evidence of Love.*

❑ Your Seed is the only proof that you have conquered greed. It will be God's biggest memory of you today.

❑ Receiving establishes your limits. *Sowing takes the limits off.* That's why Jesus said that it is more *advantageous* and *productive to give...* than to receive. When you unleash your seed... you unleash the potential of your *future*.

WISDOM FROM THE WORD

"...It is more blessed to give, than to receive."
Acts 20:35b

DAY
31

GIVE YOUR SEED TIME TO GROW.

❏ Don't get weary in waiting. There is *always* a due season.

❏ There is always a *distance* between your sowing season and your reaping season. It will require your faith. *That is what impresses God.*

❏ Champions e*ndure. This is how they become champions.*

WISDOM FROM THE WORD

"And let us not be weary in well doing: for in due season we shall reap, if we faint not."
Galatians 6:9

Decision Page

Will You Accept Jesus As Savior Of Your Life Today?

The Bible says, "That if thou shalt confess with thy mouth the Lord Jesus, and shall believe in thine heart that God hath raised Him from the dead, thou shalt be saved. For with the heart man believeth unto righteousness; and with the mouth confession is made unto salvation."(Rom. 10:9-10)

To receive Jesus Christ as Lord and Savior of your life, please pray this prayer from your heart today!

"Dear Jesus, I believe that you died for me and rose again on the third day. I confess I am a sinner. I need Your love and forgiveness. Come into my life, forgive my sins, and give me eternal life. I confess You now as my Lord. Thank You for my salvation, Your peace and joy. Amen."

Return This Today!

❑ Yes, Mike! I made a decision to accept Christ as my personal Savior today. Please send me my free gift copy of your book "31 Keys To A New Beginning" to help me with my new life in Christ. (B48)

"Sow A Seed Of Wisdom Into The Lives Of Those You Love!"

Here is your opportunity to invest in the lives of your Love Circle. Purchase 2 copies of *Seeds of Wisdom On Seed-Faith* for only $5 for 2 special people in your life. These dynamic daily devotionals are your answer to the "Daily Bread" of the Wisdom of God.

❑ Yes, Mike, I want to Sow 2 *Seeds of Wisdom On Seed-Faith* into 2 people that I love. I have enclosed $5 for the 2 books. Please rush them immediately. (SOW048)

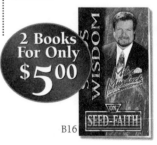

B16

Send A Self-Addressed Envelope With Check Or Money Order To: Mike Murdock
P.O. Box 99 • Dallas, TX • 75221